HAL•LEONARD
INSTRUMENTAL
PLAY-ALONG

AUDIO
ACCESS
INCLUDED

PLAYBACK+
Speed • Pitch • Balance • Loop

VIOLIN

CHRISTMAS CLASSICS

T0065900

Audio arrangements by Peter Deneff

To access audio visit:
www.halleonard.com/mylibrary

Enter Code
4141-4608-4006-7689

ISBN 978-1-4950-7061-7

HAL•LEONARD®
CORPORATION
7777 W. BLUEMOUND RD. P.O. BOX 13819 MILWAUKEE, WI 53213

In Australia Contact:
Hal Leonard Australia Pty. Ltd.
4 Lentara Court
Cheltenham, Victoria, 3192 Australia
Email: ausadmin@halleonard.com.au

Visit Hal Leonard Online at
www.halleonard.com

ANGELS WE HAVE HEARD ON HIGH

VIOLIN

Traditional French Carol

BRING A TORCH, JEANNETTE, ISABELLA

VIOLIN

17th Century French Provençal Carol

COVENTRY CAROL

VIOLIN

Traditional English Melody

FUM, FUM, FUM

VIOLIN

Traditional Catalonian Carol

GO, TELL IT ON THE MOUNTAIN

VIOLIN

African-American Spiritual

GOD REST YE MERRY, GENTLEMEN

VIOLIN

Traditional English Carol

HERE WE COME A-CAROLING

VIOLIN

Traditional

THE HOLLY AND THE IVY

VIOLIN

18th Century English Carol

rit. e dim.

I SAW THREE SHIPS

VIOLIN

Traditional English Carol

JINGLE BELLS

Words and Music by
J. PIERPONT

VIOLIN

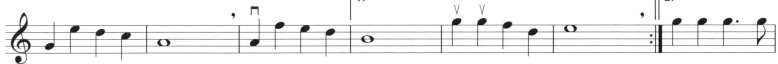

O COME, ALL YE FAITHFUL

VIOLIN

Music by JOHN FRANCIS WADE

O HOLY NIGHT

VIOLIN

French Words by PLACIDE CAPPEAU
English Words by JOHN S. DWIGHT
Music by ADOLPHE ADAM

SILENT NIGHT

VIOLIN

Words by JOSEPH MOHR
Music by FRANZ X. GRUBER

STILL, STILL, STILL

VIOLIN

Salzburg Melody, c.1819

WHAT CHILD IS THIS?

VIOLIN

16th Century English Melody